NEGOTIATION SKILLS FOR MANAGERS

NEGOTIATION SKILLS FOR MANAGERS

Series " Management Skills for Managers "
By: D.K. Hawkins
Version 1.1 ~September 2021
Published by D.K. Hawkins at KDP
Copyright ©2021 by D.K. Hawkins. All rights reserved.

No part of this publication may be reproduced, distributed or transmitted in any form or by any means including photocopying, recording or other electronic or mechanical methods or by any information storage or retrieval system without the prior written permission of the publishers, except in the case of very brief quotations embodied in critical reviews and certain other noncommercial uses permitted by copyright law.

All rights reserved, including the right of reproduction in whole or in part in any form.

All information in this book has been carefully researched and checked for factual accuracy. However, the author and publisher make no warranty, express or implied, that the information contained herein is appropriate for every individual, situation, or purpose and assume no responsibility for errors or omissions.

The reader assumes the risk and full responsibility for all actions. The author will not be held responsible for any loss or damage, whether consequential, incidental, special, or otherwise, that may result from the information presented in this book.

All images are free for use or purchased from stock photo sites or royalty-free for commercial use. I have relied on my own observations as well as many different sources for this book, and I have done my best to check facts and give credit where it is due. In the event that any material is used without proper permission, please contact me so that the oversight can be corrected.

The information provided in this book is for informational purposes only and is not intended to be a source of advice or credit analysis with respect to the material presented. The information and/or documents contained in this book do not constitute legal or financial advice and should never be used without first consulting with a financial professional to determine what may be best for your individual needs.

The publisher and the author do not make any guarantee or other promise as to any results that may be obtained from using the content of this book. You should never make any investment decision without first consulting with your own financial advisor and conducting your own research and due diligence. To the maximum extent permitted by law, the publisher and the author disclaim any and all liability in the event any information, commentary, analysis, opinions, advice and/or recommendations contained in this book prove to be inaccurate, incomplete or unreliable, or result in any investment or other losses.

Content contained or made available through this book is not intended to and does not constitute legal advice or investment advice and no attorney-client relationship is formed. The publisher and the author are providing this book and its contents on an "as is" basis. Your use of the information in this book is at your own risk.

TABLE OF CONTENTS.

TABLE OF CONTENTS. 3
INTRODUCTION 5
CHAPTER 1 9
    How Is Negotiation Defined? 9
CHAPTER 2 14
    The Advantages of Effective Negotiation for Managers. 14
CHAPTER 3 21
    Conditions For Successful Negotiations. 21
CHAPTER 4 27
    Distinct Forms Of Negotiating Styles. 27
CHAPTER 5 32
    The Principles Of The Negotiating Process. 32
CHAPTER 6 36
    Influencing Factors For Effective Negotiation. 36
CHAPTER 7 40
    Effective Communication Skills For Effective Negotiation. ... 40
CHAPTER 8 44
    Training in Leadership Development and Negotiation. 44
CHAPTER 9 48
    Important Negotiation Skills For Dealing With Complex Negotiations. 48

CHAPTER 10 55
   Guidelines For Developing Effective Negotiation Techniques.
   55
CHAPTER 11 61
   The Best Negotiation Advice For Managers. 61
CONCLUSION. 66

INTRODUCTION.

There are some abilities that one must possess to be successful in life. These abilities can vary according to your goals. There are occasions in life when you will find yourself in a managerial role.

You are expected to have some amount of vision and character as a leader/manager. These, along with other positive leadership characteristics, will help you establish a reputation as a knowledgeable and respectable leader.

Another important role is played by people responsible for negotiating. Individuals who work as negotiators must have a clear understanding of their roles and different characteristics. Negotiations often occur in business. For example, to ensure that some conversations run successfully, one must possess the qualities necessary to please all parties.

Some individuals ask if there is a connection between the concepts of leadership and negotiating. In summary, there is a clear connection between the two. You cannot negotiate effectively if you lack the necessary leadership abilities.

It is not always true that all leaders/managers are excellent negotiators. Also, it is not true that negotiators possess outstanding leadership characteristics. What is true is that to succeed in either capacity and accomplish the objectives you set, you must possess a few key characteristics of a leader. If you find yourself in control of a group of people, there are some basic attributes of a leader that you must possess.

Vision is among the most significant characteristics that one must possess. It is important to be some that you understand what you desire. You need to understand what you desire, but it is also important for you to educate others. If you are in control of a team, you need to communicate your vision or the team's vision to which you belong.

There are many ways to communicate your team's vision. You must use your words to create an image. Declare it aloud, type it up or even sketch it out. You can create this image in any way that works for you.

Consider soliciting feedback from team members regarding their perceptions of the team's vision. This is to ascertain the clarity with which you have communicated your overarching objective. This assists in ensuring that they understand your intentions, ensuring that you are all on the same page.

The great majority of discussions do not end in the manner in which the parties desire. Negotiation may be a lengthy and arduous process, and in such instances, both parties may become disinterested and lose the desire to continue. Also, a lack of motivation on either of the persons can quickly result in a collapse, effectively ending any future possibility of an agreement.

Occasionally, a third party can arrange a contract with your suppliers or customers more quickly than you can, and given that 'there is no point in weeping over spilled milk,' why would you want that to happen?

Negotiation is not something to avoid, but it should be a last resort when it is clear that the process would be ineffective. For instance, if prior negotiations with one of your suppliers or clients did not result in a satisfactory outcome, cease negotiating and try something different.

If you had the opportunity to routinely convert your negotiation opportunities into "get more" scenarios - and so stay well ahead of the game, wouldn't you jump at the chance?

Continue reading to learn many effective charismatic techniques for dramatically raising the bar in your favor.

CHAPTER 1

How Is Negotiation Defined?

Negotiation is an interactive social process in which individuals engage with another person or parties to establish an agreement on their behalf. Negotiation is primarily used to ensure that one's expectations of others are met. It is a method of communication used to reach an agreement when two or more parties have similar interests and others that are opposed.

According to the Shorter Oxford Dictionary, 1977-Negotiation: To confer with another to resolve some difficulties amicably; to debate a matter to reach an agreement or compromise.

As Ginny Pearsom Bames defines negotiation as the process of settling a problem by giving and taking within the context of a specific relationship. It comprises exchanging ideas and facts and striving to establish a mutually agreeable agreement.

In the United States of America, Pepperdine University has proposed the following explanation for the term "negotiation": A negotiation is a communication method used to close deals and resolve disputes.

It is a voluntary, non-binding process in which the parties retain control over both the agreement's outcome and the procedures used to attain it. Due to the fact that the majority of parties place narrow limits on the negotiation process, it offers a varied range of possible options, increasing the likelihood of joint benefit.

As defined by Williams in Legal and Settlement 1983, negotiation is a recurring process that generally exhibits predictable patterns across time. Yet, in legal conflicts, the attorney's focus and energy are diverted so much by the pre-trial procedure and trial strategy that they fail to grasp the important identifiable patterns and dynamics of the negotiating process.

M Anstey summarizes the fundamental components of negotiation as follows:

1. An interactive verbal procedure
2. Involving two or more parties
3. Seeking agreement
4. Over a disagreement or conflict of interest between them
5. They endeavor to preserve their respective interests while adjusting their ideas and positions in the joint effort to reach an agreement.

Negotiation, in broad terms, is an interaction of influences. These interactions might take the form of settling disagreements, agreeing on courses of action, negotiating for individual or group interests, or constructing solutions that satisfy multiple interests. Thus, negotiation is an alternate method of resolving disputes (ADR).

Negotiation Characteristics:

Negotiation is a process involving more than two parties who require (or believe they require) each other's engagement to achieve the desired conclusion. The parties share a common interest.

1) The parties begin with divergent perspectives or goals. These distinctions are what prevent agreement.

2) The parties are willing to collaborate and communicate to accomplish their objectives.

3) By influencing one another, the parties can mutually profit or prevent harm.

4) The parties recognize that any other course of action will fail to accomplish the desired result.

5) The parties believe that negotiation is the best (or at the very least a possible) method of resolving their disputes.

6) They also believe that they may persuade the other party to modify their initial position.

7) Even if they do not obtain their desired outcome, both keep optimism for a satisfactory outcome.

8) Each has some real or perceived influence over the behavior of the other. If one party is powerless, the other party will find negotiation pointless.

9) The negotiation process itself entails interpersonal interaction. This encounter may occur in person, via telephone, letter, or any combination thereof; yet, emotions and attitudes will always play a role because it is personal.

CHAPTER 2

The Advantages of Effective Negotiation for Managers.

Suppose you're interested in the benefits of excellent negotiation skills. In that case, you're probably a manager seeking to enhance your talents, a shy individual tired of being at the bottom of the food chain, or the type of person who enjoys learning new things.

Few individuals recognize that negotiating is a virtually daily occurrence; the only thing that distinguishes negotiation from "making a deal" is the affected parties' perceived importance.

What are effective negotiation skills?

We'll approach this issue more seriously than negotiating. "You may go out Friday night if you mow the yard."

A competent negotiator must be intelligent; this does not necessarily imply that you have an IQ comparable to Einstein's; the opposite is true in certain circumstances. A person must be intelligent enough to see that they are either ignorant of the subject, which is nothing to be ashamed of, or their opponent dwarfs everything except fools.

One must be willing to conduct research and exercise due diligence to understand the subject thoroughly and have the ability to comprehend and discuss an opponent's proposals intelligently. To be an effective negotiator, one must learn human emotions and behavior and discern the opponent is experiencing, when, and why.

Negotiations, in theory, should always be emotionless; the "can't take it personally" approach should always prevail. However, who is negotiating; humans and humans. Both have emotions, which some are better at controlling or concealing than others but all experience.

By evaluating your opponent, which a skilled negotiator would do in advance to elicit responses to specific questions or scenarios, you may put yourself in your opponent's shoes, which may provide insight into his motivations and how to handle them.

A great negotiator will preserve an honest and fair reputation, which does not imply weakness. Many inexperienced or arrogant individuals placed in the position of negotiating a matter or contract will maintain an adamant position of wanting everything their way, from all their demands to the temperature set on the air conditioner, which only serves to create an adversarial, confrontational atmosphere.

Simple concerns will gradually escalate into tremendous obstacles. It will swiftly devolve into an "I'll take my ball and go home" situation, in which everyone digs their respective heels in and refuses to bend.

The great negotiator understands that to reach an agreement that both sides can live with, he must finally provide a win-win situation and do everything possible to avoid creating a combative atmosphere.

I was previously involved in a series of contract negotiations that had reached a standstill. The ground rules stipulated that any request for a recess must be made alternately; in other words, once a break was granted, the corporation could not request another until the union had used one.

I was taken aback when the union chief negotiator abruptly sought a recess, and we sat at the table doing nothing. When the company's human resource manager re-entered the room, the union spokesman inquired about his well-being. "Good," answered the union spokesman, "I could see you weren't feeling well, so I called a recess." The gentleman appeared astonished and nodded his head in agreement.

"I had a lousy lunch," the man said. From that point forward, because one negotiator prioritized the well-being of the other over the importance of the contract negotiations, the stalemate was broken, and negotiations were swiftly resolved.

In the commercial sector, having effective negotiation skills might mean the difference between success and failure. Those that are adept in negotiating often rise to the top of their respective industries.

Simultaneously, individuals who cannot negotiate prefer to remain where they are or fall backward. If you aspire to be successful in the industry, you should prioritize honing your negotiating abilities.

Consider the following points regarding the important nature of effective negotiation skills to your organization's success as a manager.

One of the key advantages of having effective negotiation abilities is the ability to save money. If you represent your firm or are negotiating on your behalf, you can bargain for a lower price while purchasing something.

When making significant purchases, you must be able to negotiate a lower deal with the salesperson. If you accept the price offered, it is highly likely that you will be taken advantage of. Learning to negotiate will enable you to save significant amounts of money over time.

Another significant benefit of acquiring strong negotiating abilities is that you will increase revenue for your organization. If you want to sell a product or secure a contract, you must be able to negotiate. This will enable you to get a higher selling price and boost your profit margins.

Along with becoming a more skilled negotiator, you will develop various other business-related characteristics. Many of the negotiation abilities you develop will transfer to other aspects of your organization.

For instance, developing great negotiation skills teaches you how to be an effective listener. To negotiate well, you must listen to the other party and determine what they want. This ability will prove extremely useful in other areas of the business.

You must listen to your staff to ascertain their motivations. When dealing with customers, you must listen to their needs to find a product or service that meets their demands.

When it comes to company success, acquiring strong negotiation skills should be a key concern. This is by far the most important talent that a businessperson can develop. It can effortlessly transport you from your current location to your desired destination.

CHAPTER 3

Conditions For Successful Negotiations.

Many variables influence the success or failure of negotiations. The following conditions increase the likelihood of success in negotiations:

Parties:

Parties who are identified and willing to participate: If fruitful negotiations occur, the individuals or organizations with a stake in the outcome must be identifiable and willing to sit down at the negotiating table. Suppose a significant partner is either missing or unwilling to negotiate good faith, and the likelihood of reaching an agreement decreases.

Interdependence:

Interdependence: For meaningful talks to occur, players must rely on one another to address their needs or interests. To satisfy their interests, the players require either one another's support or inhibition from negative behavior. If one party can fulfill his or her demands without the other's involvement, there will be little incentive to negotiate.

People:

People must be willing to compromise for communication to begin. When participants aren't psychologically prepared to speak with the other party, when sufficient information is unavailable, or a negotiating plan is not established, players may hesitate to begin the process.

Influence or leverage:

Influence or leverage: For individuals to agree on contentious subjects, they must possess some methods of influencing other negotiators' attitudes and/or actions. Often, influence is equated with the ability to threaten or inflict pain or undesired consequences, although this is one method of persuading someone to change.

Posing provocative questions, offering necessary information, soliciting expert advice, appealing to a party's prominent associates, exercising legitimate authority, or providing rewards are all ways to exert influence during talks.

Agreement on some interests and issues: For discussions to progress, parties must agree on shared interests and issues. In general, participants will share some concerns and interests and have others exclusive to one party.

The number and significance of common concerns and interests affect whether conversations occur and conclude in agreement. Parties must share a sufficient number of issues and interests to commit to a collaborative decision-making process.

Participants must have a desire to settle for talks to work. If resolving a disagreement is more important than resolving it, then discussions will fail.

Often, parties wish to prolong conflicts to retain a relationship (even a negative one may be preferable to no relationship at all), organize public opinion or support in their favor, or give their lives meaning through the conflicted relationship. These variables contribute to the continuation of division and work against the resolution.

The unpredictability of outcome: Individuals bargain to obtain something from another. Also, they bargain since the consequences of not negotiating are unpredictable.

For instance, if a person believes that going to court will result in a 50/50 chance of winning, s/he may choose to negotiate rather than risk losing due to a judicial ruling.

Negotiation is more predictable than court because good negotiation results in a party gaining something. For parties to enter into negotiations, the chances of a decisive and one-sided win must be unpredictable.

A sense of urgency and a deadline: Negotiations typically occur when there is a sense of urgency or when a decision must be made quickly. External or internal time restrictions and potential negative or positive effects of a negotiation decision can induce urgency.

External limitations may include court dates, impending executive or administrative judgments, or predicted changes in the external environment. A negotiator may impose internal restraints to increase the motivation of another to settle.

To be successful in negotiations, participants must have a sense of urgency and be aware that they may face severe consequences or loss of benefits if a timely conclusion is not made.

There are no significant psychological impediments to settlement: Strong feelings about another party, whether voiced or unspoken, can significantly affect a person's psychological preparedness to deal. Psychological obstacles to the settlement must be overcome for successful talks to take place.

Negotiable issues: To conduct a successful negotiation, negotiators must think that acceptable settlement possibilities are attainable due to their participation in the process. If it looks that discussions will only result in a win/lose outcome and that a party's needs will be unmet due to involvement, parties may be hesitant to engage in communication.

CHAPTER 4

Distinct Forms Of Negotiating Styles.

How you negotiate is also a strategy. There are many negotiating styles. On occasion, the style represents the party's attitude, and an experienced negotiator can forecast the outcome based on the party's behavior as revealed by the style.

The negotiation style is represented in the negotiators' communication abilities, interpersonal conduct, language, tone of voice, choices, listening ability, non-verbal gestures, and judgment. Generally, three distinct forms of negotiating styles exist. The following is a brief description:

- Collaborative Approach:

Typical methods employed in this negotiating style include making concessions, providing information, and adopting fair and acceptable conduct. Thus, a cooperative negotiator often explains her concessions and ideas and attempts to reconcile the parties' opposing interests; her proposals are evaluated against standards on which both parties may agree, such as the legal merits of the case and the parties' fairness.

The advantage of a cooperative negotiation style is that it results in fewer breaks in negotiating and subsequent recourse to litigation and more advantageous outcomes for both parties. This puts both clients and negotiators back in a position to 'do business.'

However, the cooperative manner is susceptible to operational challenges when the parties to the negotiation are uneven in money or power or when one party refuses to bargain for joint or mutual gain.

- Competitor's Attitude:

Thus, the competitive negotiator makes hesitant concessions to avoid 'weakening his position' through position or image loss. He often makes unreasonable first demands, makes few concessions, and generally has a high level of aspiration for his customer.

It is often asserted that this style leads practitioners to adopt specific negotiation strategies. These strategies could be never making the initial offer, always attempting to conceal the client's true objectives, always being the one who drafts the final offer, the use of exaggeration, threat, and bluff to instill high levels of tension and pressure on the opponent.

When utilized properly, these strategies cause the opposing party to lose confidence in their argument and lower their expectations for the outcome for their client. Thus, it is a purely manipulative strategy to intimidate the opposite party into adopting a negotiator's demands.

- Approach to Problem Solving:

A problem-solving approach to an access disagreement may be founded on the notion that, while both parents desire access to their children for a portion of the day, neither would desire access for the entire time. On this basis, a beneficial solution to all parties (including the children) can be arranged.

Thus, the problem-solving technique begins with both negotiators attempting to uncover their clients' underlying needs.

This is best accomplished through client interviews in which the lawyer discusses with the client how he wishes to resolve the conflict in social, economic, ethical, and psychological aspects. Focusing on clients' actual needs results in more complex solutions than those arising from competitive negotiation.

Fisher and Ury identify four fundamental approaches as being important to the problem-solving negotiating process. They are as follows:

1. Distinguish people from problems; In other words, disentangle the interpersonal interaction between negotiators and their customers from the merits of the problem or disagreement.

2. Put clients' interests first; that is, evaluate the clients' interests so that each party's reasons, aims, and values are well understood.

3. Generate different possibilities; for instance, conduct a brainstorming session to generate new ideas that address the parties' concerns.

4. Insist on an objective criterion for the conclusion of the negotiation; that is, evaluate suggested outcomes against readily ascertainable standards based on objective criteria.

CHAPTER 5

The Principles Of The Negotiating Process.

It is crucial to recognize that the negotiation process follows some fundamental structures. These structures improve the negotiator's competence and talents and create a thriving environment conducive to productive negotiation. The most fundamental system is as follows:

Agenda-setting:

Unless a schedule has been agreed upon in advance, you will agree with the opposing lawyer on the practical details of how the negotiation will be handled, the agenda for the conversations, and how the discussions will be recorded.

Accurate representation of the facts:

A feasible first step is for you or your opponent to identify and agree on the dispute's relevant available facts and the applicable legislation. This could be followed by your identification and agreement on any missing or contradictory information or paperwork discrepancies. At this point, you might attempt to resolve the disagreement by conducting an additional inquiry and listening to and interrogating the order side.

Assessment and repositioning:

You will then evaluate different solutions in light of the mutual interests of both sides (a collaborative problem-solving technique), or you will make powerful counter-proposals to your adversary's viewpoint (competitive style)

You will remove unworkable proposals (collaborative problem-solving style) or employ a range of negotiating strategies to strengthen your position and undermine your adversary's (confrontational style)

You will develop new proposals (using a collaborative problem-solving approach) or discover trade-offs and concessions (competitive style)

You will consider terminating the negotiation if the trade-offs are unacceptable to both parties (cooperative problem-solving technique) or if the trade-offs are acceptable to one party but not to the other (competitive style)

You must devise a strategy for concluding the negotiation. At this point, you have the following options: - Adjourning to acquire additional information and instructions from your client - Adjourning to tell your client of a final offer from the other side and to solicit his instructions

Reaching a formal agreement with your client's authorization

If the conclusion is favorable and a settlement is achieved, you must compare your understanding of the settlement to that of your opponent to ensure that you are on the same page. Following that, you must decide how the settlement will be legally enforceable (if at all) and who would prepare the terms of any written settlement.

Review:

Throughout the entire procedure outlined above, it is beneficial for the lawyers to periodically assess the stage reached in the conversations. This is primarily suggested if you appear to have reached a stalemate or if there is an awkward silence.

A review enables each party to assess their initial objective based on what has been accomplished thus far and choose how the negotiation should proceed. This may result in one or both negotiators expressing a revised or more inventive viewpoint as a possible solution to the problem.

CHAPTER 6

Influencing Factors For Effective Negotiation.

Many influencing factors or negotiation aspects are necessary and play an essential part in effective negotiation. The following is a brief description:

Mediator: Many elements influence the negotiation process. The first of these factors is the negotiator's talent and aptitude and his character and credibility. Another ability that is important in negotiation is the negotiator's capacity to maintain control over the process.

A negotiator should monitor the negotiation process's progress and make repeated attempts to develop bridges between the parties. They should make an effort to instill a favorable attitude toward agreement.

Controlling the entire negotiation process requires a high level of expertise and experience, which can be achieved by closely observing other parties' methods, prior knowledge, and studying the best negotiating techniques in the contemporary world.

Parties:

The parties significantly influence the negotiating process. The process is determined by the parties, their interests, and their reactions and responses. When parties to a dispute get to the negotiating table, they each bring their mindset.

Team selection:

The negotiation team should be selected based on the facts and circumstances so that each member contributes to the goal's achievement through productive labor.

Location of the negotiation:

Location of the negotiation: Occasionally, the location of the negotiation is significant. In comparison to a familiar environment, unfamiliar settings may induce stress to the opposing side.

Room arrangement:

To some extent, the room layout affects how the negotiation is conducted. In an ideal world, the layout would be determined by the circumstances in which the parties operate.

For instance, if the discussion is about a labor issue, negotiators should ensure that the distance between the sides is not excessive. Seating choices should promote a calm atmosphere. The layout should reflect the parties' views and perceptions and the problems being discussed throughout the negotiation.

Negotiation psychology:

Negotiation psychology: The psychology of the negotiators and the parties is important to the negotiating process. Individuals involved in the process bring different attitudes, approaches, and actions to the table.

Maslows' 'Need Hierarchy Theory' states that their needs influence people's behavior. He categorizes human requirements into five categories: physical and survival needs; security and safety needs; social needs; ego needs; and self-realization needs.

CHAPTER 7

Effective Communication Skills For Effective Negotiation.

Effective negotiation requires effective communication. Communication requires three important abilities: speaking, listening, and comprehension. You cannot have one talent function properly without the others.

For example, you cannot have high comprehension without good hearing and speaking skills. Negotiation is most effective when participants can articulate and explain their points of contention and misunderstanding.

Speaking:

Negotiation begins with a short, unambiguous description of the issue from each party's perspective.

Facts and emotions are presented rationally from the standpoint of the individual, utilizing "I" statements.

When comments such as "I become very upset when you" are used instead of more confrontational remarks such as "You make me angry when you," which blames the other person and puts them on the defensive, communication between people will flow more smoothly. Shared concerns, rather than individual problems, remain the focal point of conversation throughout the negotiation process.

The negotiating process will be most productive if participants take the time to consider their responses—schedule meetings in advance to ensure that everyone has a convenient time and location. A neutral, peaceful location with few distractions or interruptions is ideal for candid communication.

Listening is an active procedure that entails focusing one's full attention on the other person. Encourage the other person to share thoughts and feelings, provide comments on what was heard and keep eye contact are all abilities that demonstrate your interest in comprehending what they have to say.

It is always beneficial to just inquire, "Did I understand you correctly?" or "Did I hear you correctly that you are that way you feel?" Active listening demonstrates that the other person is being heard, welcomed, and valued. Active listening enables open, continuing negotiation.

Thinking forward or anticipating the discussion's outcome are both distractions that impair listening. Inadequate attention and listening skills can result in misconceptions, ineffective solutions, and ongoing conflict.

Before two parties seeking answers, a common understanding must be formed. If two people do not comprehend one another's difficulties and concerns, the negotiating process will either break down or ineffective solutions. Active listening fosters comprehension. It is essential to pay great attention to both what someone says and how they behave.

Body language, which includes facial expressions, hand gestures, and eye contact intensity, can convey information about another person's thoughts and feelings. However, observations are shaped equally by the observer and the observed.

It is a good habit never to assume that another person understands you without first inquiring, "Did I hear you correctly?" or "I noted your appearance" or "I sense you're stressed." "Would you like to discuss this?" and "I'd like to hear how you're feeling." "are all excellent examples of comments that promote dialogue and mutual understanding.

CHAPTER 8

Training in Leadership Development and Negotiation.

Negotiation is an important component of management and leadership. It may be necessary for different scenarios during your management career. As a result, it is essential to have a thorough understanding of negotiation and conduct successful negotiations.

Many leadership development and management development courses demonstrate how to maneuver and negotiate with other parties. It is vital to learn negotiation skills if you wish to be a good manager and leader. These abilities will help you communicate with colleagues and other experts.

When commencing the negotiation process, the first step is to ascertain the relationship's possible duration. Determine how long you intend to maintain contact with the person with whom you will be negotiating.

Whether you view it as long-term, short-term, or somewhere in between, how you approach the negotiation process will depend on your perspective. The next stage is to examine how many options and concerns each party has.

You must identify which concerns are open for debate, how many possible resolutions exist, and how many options are accessible based on the current situation. Leadership development and management development training courses are excellent ways to build the skills necessary to manage these often difficult circumstances.

Each negotiating situation is unique. Some situations may demand you to consider the needs and desires of others. In some scenarios, a third party may be necessary to the negotiation process.

Often, a circumstance will require the third party to be visible (for example, when negotiating on behalf of other parties). Occasionally, the third party will not be required to be visible. This third party is commonly referred to as a mediator.

Negotiations, leadership experts believe, are an excellent approach to resolve disagreements, bring people together and address problems. Also, experts assert that negotiation skills are essential in every managerial or supervisory function. This is true for all types of organizations' human resources.

Individuals in leadership positions must possess this ability since collaboration from all stakeholders is important to accomplishing significant goals and organizing them. Completing management development training is one approach to assist future managers and leaders in establishing this talent.

Another important component of negotiation management is that it may be utilized effectively as a management tool in the workplace to expedite the completion of tasks.

This works because negotiating gives employees a sense of ownership over the process instead of merely being told what to do. When employees are asked questions and allowed to ask their own, daily work becomes easier because they understand (through negotiation) that there is something in it.

According to experts in leadership development and management development training, negotiation is an important management technique that results in a more productive workplace.

If you understand how to employ this instrument properly, you can ensure your career and future success. Developing negotiation abilities takes time and practice, and this is a talent that requires ongoing attention to maintain proficiency.

CHAPTER 9

Important Negotiation Skills For Dealing With Complex Negotiations.

As a manager, do you ever find yourself unable to make sense of all the issues and interests of the several parties participating in a negotiation?

This is a frequent occurrence. Much has been written on negotiating in complex situations. Regrettably, the majority of it is wide in scope and fails to address the needs of business negotiators.

Business-to-business negotiation can be a very complex area. Without a navigational tool to assist you in navigating this complexity, you risk missing opportunities and paying a high price for yourself and your organization.

The key to extracting maximum value from your complex negotiation conditions is to identify and comprehend the interests of all parties affected by or involved in the discussion.

In some instances, it may be straightforward for you to comprehend participants' perspectives and interests in a discussion. However, in most cases, it is challenging to define stakeholders' interests; it is also challenging to identify all stakeholders.

What are the most critical strategies and competencies, then, for successfully resolving complicated, multi-party negotiations?

1. Identify all of the negotiation's stakeholders.

This may seem self-evident, yet it can be challenging to identify and track all parties during a discussion. At the very least, in a corporate environment, you should attempt to identify the following stakeholders:

a. The financial stakeholders

Depending on the financial terms presented, these individuals or groups will finance, underwrite, or lend authority to finalize a deal. You must identify all potential individuals interested in the financial parts of the discussion.

b. Stakeholders representing the use and or the consumer.

These are the individuals or organizations that will implement and support the agreement's outcome. These are typically the parties who will have to live and work with the result of the discussions daily.

c. Stakeholders on the technological and legal fronts

These individuals or groups will sign off on and approve the negotiations' technical and contractual aspects.

d. Guides/Gurus and Other Influential Figures

These are the individuals or groups that wield significant influence over the negotiation's decision-makers.

2. Identify the negotiating interests of each party.

There are essentially two approaches to determine an individual's or group's negotiating interest in a negotiation. The first technique is to put yourself in the shoes of that individual or group and attempt to see things from their perspective.

What other information would you require?

Which precedents would be applicable?

What hypotheses are possible to make and test?

The second method is to pose a series of questions to the individual or group to assist you (and them) in identifying their primary interests. The most crucial question is "Why?"

"Why are you so invested in this negotiation?

Why are you taking on this role?

Why is this possibility being considered?"

3. Develop a suitable frame for each stakeholder.

After identifying the stakeholder's interests, you should now design a suitable frame. Individuals make choices for different reasons. It is not appropriate to emphasize the same themes to all stakeholders to facilitate decision-making. Your primary objective should be to communicate the most relevant framing to each stakeholder or potential stakeholder.

The frame you establish for the stakeholder can significantly impact a decision or portion of a decision.

4. Establish an efficient negotiation management system

It is necessary to consider how you will manage the negotiation's diverse stakeholders. In complicated deals, you'll require different materials to assist with the negotiations. It is vital to define a clear function for each member and create an environment where you can send a consistent message to your counterparts.

If your counterparties see you and your team as reasonable, the likelihood that they will respond rationally to you increases significantly.

You can only present a cohesive and coherent 'front' if you have evaluated your negotiation team's duties and responsibilities.

Divide the team's focus between those responsible for relationship management and those responsible for or engaging in task-related tasks. Remember that you must develop a schedule that takes into account the interests of all potential stakeholders.

The structure is an effective technique for you to simplify complex negotiations.

You must concentrate on the process factors to make progress at each stage of the negotiation. You will discover that complexity can be more easily managed when a suitable supporting structure is used.

CHAPTER 10

Guidelines For Developing Effective Negotiation Techniques.

Never engage in any deal or negotiation in a desperate state of mind. When you demonstrate your desperation, you deprive yourself of negotiating leverage. Your appetite and perceived desire will detract from the transaction's worth.

Other than that, take a step back, collect your thoughts and reschedule the meetings. Often, we assign value to products depending on our requirements. Nobody wishes to spend more than the product's or services' true value.

As managers, we have underestimated the value of effective negotiation, resulting in a waste of time, value, and resources. Whereas we could have harvested millions, we settled for a few thousand dollars, which may cover a few bills and kick-start an economy.

The question is whether we sufficiently calculate, plan and prepare for discussions, bargains or agreements or whether we view the dotted line as the red sea's celebration, an impending breakthrough, and overlook the small print.

I've watched with fascination as quick spurts of excitement at the signing of mergers between businesses, political organizations, and even religions have devolved into a succession of grief experiences once the dotted and signed paper is activated. Before you can have the fabled handshake to signify an agreement, you must carefully evaluate your actions.

The choices made at this moment will have a long-term impact on where your business will be soon. Recognize that individuals who have entrusted you with the job of negotiating to rely on you to make judgments in the organization's best interests.

The following are some general guidelines for negotiation.

• Conduct preliminary research and investigations on the other party before the meeting. Conduct a background check on the other party's trade references and the outcomes of previous agreements.

Utilize your non-negotiable checklist to choose whether or not to advance with talks. It may be unnecessary to get into negotiations if the opposing side has already failed the "non-negotiable" criteria.

Solicit the assistance of a legal representative to investigate and examine contracts or agreements. • Prepare questions in advance to elicit clarification on any terms in previously received documents. Preparation requires anticipating and responding to questions before engaging.

It requires making your best case and providing alternatives when necessary, which is why it is important. There is nothing wrong with anticipating a deadlock situation and devising a strategy for breaking it.

- Attend key meetings with a witness(es) or other individuals who contribute to the conversation. This may be your Assistant or a senior member of your staff. You may require the assistance of someone who can provide pointers and suggestions.

Occasionally, when negotiating alone with a panel, you will lose based on statistics, as there may be five active brains thinking ahead of you.

- Do not rush to make a choice - Always stare squarely at the negotiating party and avoid being forced into making a decision immediately. Never should the emphasis be solely on completing the agreement without the parties accepting ownership of the decisions they are making. When there is haste, you must suspect that anything is hidden in the agreement. Allow yourself time. You are not required to sign immediately.

- Recognize the time aspect - There is always a time suited to negotiating. You cannot bargain effectively if you are rushed or if both parties are exhausted. Depending on how hot the discussions become, it is prudent to request a "time out" to regain your composure.

- Avoid emotional negotiating - Distancing yourself from the problem under discussion. When you become enraged or enthusiastic, you lose your composure and negotiating ability.

- Focus on the subject under conversation or negotiation and avoid attacking the individual- There is a propensity to address the subject's personality rather than the subject under discussion or negotiation. While it is necessary to understand the type of person you are negotiating with, the subject at hand takes precedence over personalities.

- Pay attention to detail - If you are presented with documents during a meeting without reading them beforehand, it is important to read the small print or assign a specialist on your team to scrutinize them while you speak. Typically, the fine print is the basis of all disagreements in any negotiation.

- Be prepared for compromise - Before engaging in a negotiation, you should be aware of both your best and worst-case scenarios and the advantages and disadvantages of each. , you should begin the negotiation by presenting your strongest case.

While negotiating, some concessions are necessary but not to the detriment of your worst-case situation. I've heard it said that "both parties must feel as though they gained some and lost some in a negotiation."

- Never communicate your desperation to the other side - It is important to conduct a SWOT analysis of yourself and your joining team. Once you understand your strengths, you will not allow someone who lacks in-depth knowledge of the topic at hand to drive the discussion. Avoid exposing any flaws you may have, as the opposing party may exploit them, rendering your plan ineffective.

CHAPTER 11

The Best Negotiation Advice For Managers.

In general, negotiation is contingent upon the negotiator's competence, skill, method, and knowledge. Negotiation tips vary according to a negotiator. The following are some of the best negotiating tips with examples:

- Be open to negotiating in the first place:

Some individuals are fearful of discussing money. Others believe it is impolite or insulting, and they are often correct. However, when it comes to closing a deal - as we all must do - refusing to engage in "money-talk" may be a very costly affair.

There are plenty of skilled negotiators available. If you're purchasing a house or a car or changing jobs, you can be some you'll come into contact with this type of person. If they notice your timidity in general, they will take advantage of it.

- Avoid becoming emotionally involved:

One significant error that many inexperienced negotiators make is becoming overly emotionally invested in winning. They scream, threaten and demand to be granted their wishes. All of this is counterproductive.

Most transactions are only possible if both parties believe they would benefit from them. If the individual across the table feels assaulted or dislikes you, they are unlikely to back down. Many people despise bullies and will walk away from trade if one is involved.

Maintain a calm, tolerant and friendly demeanor, even if the other person begins to lose their temper. Ensure that you check your pride and ego at the door. That way, you are more likely to succeed.

- Avoid being duped by the "rules" trick:

When someone offers me a contract to sign, I mark out anything I don't agree with. I'm also happy to add items that I believe should be included. Occasionally, the opposing party will return to me and say, "You are not permitted to make such alterations to our contracts." Is that true?

Given that I am the one signing the document, I will make any changes I desire. No legislation requires them to be the sole party permitted to amend a contract.

If they are unhappy with my adjustments, inform me, and we can work something out; do not tell me I lack authorization. This exemplifies a frequent strategy employed by skilled negotiators such as real estate agents, employment agents, and vehicle dealers. They are aware that many people are rigid about obeying rules.

As a result, they will fabricate official-sounding announcements and insist that "this is the proper way to do it" or "you are not permitted to do that."

Suppose someone attempts to suffocate you by adding regulations to the transaction, demand confirmation that such rules exist.

- Never be the first to give a figure a name:

This is a costly lesson to learn but a necessary one. I do many contract works, and one of the first questions I'm always asked is, "How much do you charge per hour?" This is a high-stakes issue, and I often found myself blurting out an answer that was less than what I want.

I've learned recently how important it is to get the other person to say a number first. Now, I react to that inquiry by inquiring, "What is the contract's budget?" Often, I am shocked to learn they are offering me a greater value than I anticipated.

- Request more than you expect to receive: Once the other party has provided their amount, even if it is significantly higher than you anticipated, say something along the lines of "I believe you'll have to do better than that." Avoid arrogance and aggression. State it quietly.

When they inquire about your expectations, request more than what you anticipate receiving. Few individuals will walk away from a negotiation once it has begun, and you can give the other party the impression that they are winning by gradually lowering your "unrealistic expectations."

- implying that you're willing to walk away can work wonders in terms of securing a better offer. Always assume the role of the hesitant customer or seller.

CONCLUSION.

Good negotiation abilities can boost your credibility, your communication, and your business. These simple steps discussed so far in this book will make all the difference.

Begin with a clear knowledge of what you want from the negotiation. Dig below the surface. If you are negotiating a higher sale price or a reduction, you could become caught on a line item; instead, consider the overall picture.

Creativity may result in you receiving a holiday after a conference - with your client covering the cost of your travel to the event. Alternatively, you might acquire an ownership stake in a business as part of your remuneration for a potential long-term return. When you are clear on your short- and long-term goals, you are in a strong position to negotiate.

Declare your purpose to engage in a win-win discussion from the start. Eliminate any potential hostile positioning by directly addressing it. You may remark, "I'd want to address a few additional areas where I'd like to see improvements.

My objective is that we strike an unquestionably fair deal for both of us. Is that acceptable?" Before continuing, agree on the purpose of the debate and the basic rules for transparency and impartiality.

Inquire about the other party's underlying needs. As you presumably found in the preceding stage, there may be many important aspects that require consideration. If you were negotiating real estate acquisition, you might inquire about the sellers' financial intentions.

Whether they had already purchased another property or desired continued financial flow from an investment, their approach to the deal would be radically different. Continue asking questions until you have a firm grasp on what will meet their needs. You are now prepared to go to the next phase.

Be adaptable in satisfying the needs of both parties while making minimal sacrifices. After completing these steps discussed earlier, you should have a sizable list of possibilities, and now it's time to be creative.

Be prepared to extend your request beyond the scope of your initial request. Make incremental concessions to keep the conversation going forward.

Never make your final offer before you've conceded many minor points. Suppose you make a final offer without properly appreciating what you are giving. In that case, you risk reaching an early impasse. It is very likely that by employing this strategy, you may obtain a significantly more beneficial agreement than you anticipated - while also satisfying the other party.

By following the four keys outlined above, you will considerably increase your chances of success during negotiations. However, if either party engages in one of the following behaviors, the negotiation is unlikely to succeed.

At times, a prior occurrence becomes a source of contention. Perhaps an event has been destroyed, or a deadline has passed. During a recent negotiation, the bride's mother reiterated her daughter's statement that she cried on her wedding day. It is crucial to recognize that YOU CANNOT CHANGE THE PAST.

The purpose of negotiation is to agree on something that exists in the present and will continue to exist in the future. Both sides must agree to explore only the possibilities that are currently open to them. Fixation on the past can be a losing strategy because it places a premium on emotion as a currency.

Negotiating to gain power or inflict suffering. In divorces and other emotionally charged situations, there is often little chance of a win-win solution, as one or both parties are interested in causing the other party misery. Money is merely a means of dispersing pain - and as a result, no one truly wins. If this occurs, return to step one. Determine your true desires and encourage the other side to do the same.

Mastering these principles demands a high level of introspection and excellent listening and communication abilities. However, they can help you develop into a competent negotiator. Not only that, excellent negotiating can help you earn the trust of others.

Thanks for Reading.

Management Skills for Managers

1. Time Management for Managers
2. Employee Coaching for Managers
3. Team Building for Managers
4. Self Confidence for Managers
5. Negotiation Skills for Managers
6. Customer Service Skills for Managers
7. Coming soon

www.ingramcontent.com/pod-product-compliance
Lightning Source LLC
Chambersburg PA
CBHW070125230526
45472CB00004B/1422